wiccan MOON
Magic

wiccan MOON
Magic

spells and rituals to harness
lunar energy for wellbeing
and joy

cerridwen greenleaf

CICO BOOKS
LONDON NEW YORK

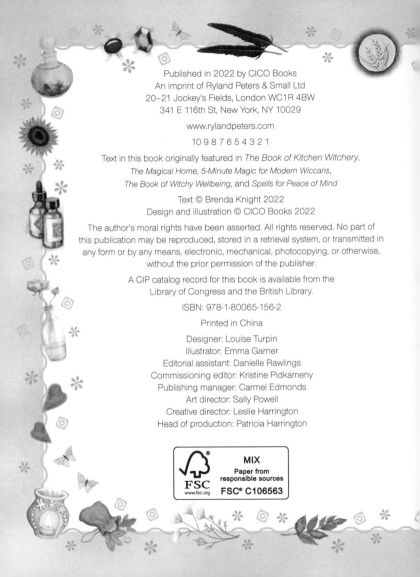

Published in 2022 by CICO Books
An imprint of Ryland Peters & Small Ltd
20–21 Jockey's Fields, London WC1R 4BW
341 E 116th St, New York, NY 10029

www.rylandpeters.com

10 9 8 7 6 5 4 3 2 1

Text in this book originally featured in *The Book of Kitchen Witchery*,
The Magical Home, *5-Minute Magic for Modern Wiccans*,
The Book of Witchy Wellbeing, and *Spells for Peace of Mind*

Text © Brenda Knight 2022
Design and illustration © CICO Books 2022

A CIP catalog record for this book is available from the
Library of Congress and the British Library.

ISBN: 978-1-80065-156-2

Printed in China

Designer: Louise Turpin
Illustrator: Emma Garner
Editorial assistant: Danielle Rawlings
Commissioning editor: Kristine Pidkameny
Publishing manager: Carmel Edmonds
Art director: Sally Powell
Creative director: Leslie Harrington
Head of production: Patricia Harrington

MIX
Paper from
responsible sources
FSC® C106563
FSC
www.fsc.org

Contents

Introduction: Let the Moon Be Your Guide

The proper phase of the moon is essential for spellcraft. Each lunar cycle begins with a "new" phase when the moon lies between the sun and the earth so the illuminated side cannot be seen from earth. The moon gradually "waxes" until it has moved to the opposite side of the earth, and its lit side faces us in the "full" moon phase. It then begins to "wane" until it reaches the new moon phase again. The entire cycle takes around a month, during which the moon orbits the earth.

Performing a spell at the optimal time in the lunar cycle will maximize your power. As you read the spells in this book, keep this essential approach to magic in mind.

HOW TO MATCH YOUR SPELLS TO MOON PHASES

• The new moon is an auspicious time for a fresh start.

• The crescent moon, which appears seven days before and after the new moon, is the time for productivity and creating positive energy.

• While waxing, the moon grows steadily larger and is good for spellwork toward completing goals and building toward an outcome.

• The full moon is a great teacher with a special message for each month.

• The waning moon is the time to wind down any personal challenges and see them to an end.

Lunar and Solar Sign Connections

When the sun or moon is in a certain zodiac sign, it carries that astrological energy. The zodiacal year starts with the sun in Aries, usually on March 21, and the sun then goes through all twelve astrological signs each month. The moon moves more quickly than the sun and stays in a sign for two days before moving on to the next. I recommend consulting a reliable source for tracking the sign of the moon—see Resources (page 142).

Timing It Well

It's a good idea to create a Book of Shadows—a journal for all your rituals, energy work, circles, spells, and all the magic you have manifested—if you do not have one already. Use your Book of Shadows for keeping track of moon phases and magical workings. Your results will show you which rituals were most successful, and when you carried them out. For example, you might have performed an autumnal Pisces Full Moon ritual with your group, and found out that your home felt wonderfully fresh for weeks afterward. That would be a strong indicator that the Pisces full moon is an auspicious time for that type of spell work, because it imbued your home with bright blessings. You will soon see a pattern emerging, and your ritual work will be all the stronger for it.

JOURNALING PROMPTS

These prompts can be useful in planning your spell work, and you may like to record your thoughts and ideas in your Book of Shadows, too.

- The new-moon phase is the time for fresh ventures, renewing, cleansing, and clearing. What seeds will you sow during this time for new beginnings?

- A waxing moon is the time for abundance, attraction, and love magic. It can also heal rifts and protect existing relationships. What do you want to attract during this time?

• The full moon shines a light on challenges in your life; now is the time to release and let go of anything causing problems. What are the issues or old patterns you should "catch and release"?

• The waning moon is a time to emphasize the positive by banishing the negative. Rid yourself of any unconstructive feelings, habits, health challenges, or thoughts; clear out the psychic clutter with the spells you have learned and replace it with good energy. What psychic clutter do you need to clear?

chapter 1

Happy Home Magic

Making room for the moon

Your home should feel like a sanctuary. You should be able to walk in the front door and immediately feel comfortable—that you are in a place of refuge, a safe haven. There will also be surprises, and that is part of what makes house magic so exciting. For example, I recently discovered that Virgo New Moons are a power phase for me, despite being the opposite of my natal moon sign. In focusing your attention on your home and the lunar phases and signs, you'll discover what might be holding you back from being utterly happy there, and you'll be able to use this wisdom to conjure pure contentment.

Sanctuary Spell: Rose-water Rite

Three simple ingredients—a pink candle, a red rose, and water—can bestow a powerful steadying and calming influence. The rose signifies beauty, love for yourself and others, blossoming, budding, the earth, your heart, and peace. The candle stands for the yellow flame of the East, unity, harmony, focus, higher intention, and the light of the soul. Water is cleansing, free flowing, affects emotions, and stands for the West. This spell can be done alone or in a group where you pass the bowl around.

TIMING: Sun or moon in Venus-ruled Libra is a sweet time to share this rite with those you care for.

Float a red rose in a clear bowl of water and light a pink candle beside the rose. With the fingers of your left hand, gently stir the water and speak aloud this blessing:

I give myself life and health, refreshing water for my spirit.

I give myself time to rest, and space to grow.

I am love.

My heart is as big as the world.

I am peace of mind.

So be it, now and always.

Altars

An altar is a physical point of focus for your rituals and should contain a collection of symbolic objects that are assembled in a meaningful manner. Altars can be created for different purposes. A house magic altar in your home provides a space where you honor the rhythms of the season and the rhythms of your own life and household, or you can set up an altar for a specific purpose—for example, nurturing your relationship.

CREATING YOUR HOUSE MAGIC ALTAR

Your house magic altar can be a low table, the top of a chest, or even a shelf. First, smudge the space with the smoke of a sage bundle or by burning sweetgrass or copal. Then cover the altar with your favorite fabric in a color you adore and place a candle in each corner. I like to use candles of many colors to represent the rainbow array of gems.

Place your chosen gems and crystals around the candles. Rose quartz is a heart stone, and fluorite is a calming crystal, so these are good options for grounding yourself, particularly if your altar is in your bedroom, as many are.

Add fresh flowers, incense you love to smell, and any objects that have special meaning for you. Some people place lovely shells or feathers they have found on their paths or while at the beach, and others use imagery that is special—a goddess statue or a star shape, perhaps.

The most important point is that your altar should be pleasing to your eye and your sensibilities. You should feel that it represents the deepest aspects of you as a person.

BLESSING YOUR HOUSE MAGIC ALTAR

Before using your altar for spellwork and rituals,
it's important to perform a rite of blessing.

TIMING: Bless your altar during a new moon.

Light the candles and incense, and say aloud:

Here burns happiness about me.

Peace and harmony are in abundance,

Here my happiness abounds.

Gems and jewels, these bones of the earth,

Bring love, prosperity, health, and mirth.

Be it ever thus that joy is the light

That here burns bright. Blessed be!

You have now consecrated your altar. It will ease your spirit at any time
and become a source of power for you. It connects you to the earth, of
which you and all gems and crystals are part, and it will connect you to
the house magic that has now entered your life. The more you use it,
the more powerful your spells will be.

Nature as an Altar

To dispel negative energy and overcome any blocks you feel are keeping you "stuck," go for a walk in the nearest park. Find a round, flat rock 6–10 in. (15–25 cm) wide, bring it home, and clean it. Landscaping rocks and paving stones at gardening stores make marvelous outdoor altars, too. This will become an altar supplied directly to you by Mother Nature, and it will have the purest energy.

TIMING: Begin by charging the stone at your home altar during a full moon. Ideally, you'll want to perform this spell three times during three consecutive full moons before you begin drawing upon the energy of your altar stone.

Light a white candle for purification, then place your hand on the stone and chant three times:

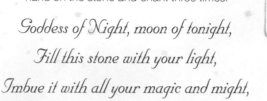

Goddess of Night, moon of tonight,

Fill this stone with your light,

Imbue it with all your magic and might,

Surround it with your protective sight.

So mote it be. Thank you, dear Goddess.

Like your home altar, your stone or nature altar will be a reservoir to which you can turn anytime you feel stuck or uninspired. Place it in your backyard or preferred outdoor space, perhaps a deck or balcony, and turn to it when you require rejuvenation. You can also specifically invoke Persephone, a goddess of spring, by placing a pomegranate on your natural altar and adding her name as the first word of the spell given above. Make sure to thank any deity you invoke in your spell work.

Stone Altar Spell: Burning Away Bad Luck

Your kitchen is the heart of your home, your sanctuary. Yet the world is constantly coming in and bringing mundane energy over your threshold—problems at the workplace, financial woes, bad news from your neighborhood or the world at large. All this negativity wants to get in the way and stay. While you can't do anything about the stock market crash in China or a co-worker's divorce, you can do something about not allowing this bad energy to cling to you by using this home-keeping spell.

TIMING: The best times to release any and all bad luck are on a Friday 13th or on any waxing moon.

Get a big black candle and a black crystal, a piece of white paper, a black pen with black ink, and a cancellation stamp, readily available at any stationery store. Go into your backyard or a nearby park or woodlands and find a flat rock that has a slightly concave surface. Using the pen, write down on the white paper that of which you want to rid yourself and your home; this is your release request. Place the candle and the black crystal on the rock; light the candle, and while it burns, intone the words of the spell opposite.

Waxing moon, most wise Selene,

From me this burden please dispel

Upon this night so clear and bright

I release ____ to the moon tonight.

Visualize a clear and peaceful home filled with only positivity as the candle burns for 13 minutes. Stamp the paper with the cancel stamp. Snuff the candle, fold the paper away from your body, and place it under the rock. Speak your thanks to the moon for assisting you. If you have a truly serious issue at hand, repeat the process for 13 nights and all will be vanquished.

Quick Tip: ALTAR BOOST
The more use an altar gets, the more energy it builds up, making your spells even more effective and powerful.

Lunar Altarations

I often switch up my altar adornments every two or three days with the changing of the lunar cycles. Here are some suggestions for altar combinations and activities in accordance with the moon phases.

New moon mini altar
Add orange candles, yellow jade, neroli essential oil, and cinnamon incense for joy, success, strength, and creativity. Write and speak goals. This is the time to let go of old ways and take up new directions.

Waxing moon mini altar
Add green candles, peridot, clary sage essential oil, and jasmine incense for prosperity, expansion, and healing. Speak your new hopes.

Half moon mini altar
Add brown candles, tiger eye, and amber oil and incense for grounding and stability. Hold your focus and feel your rootedness to Earth.

Waxing gibbous moon altar
Add red candles, garnet, and rose essential oil and incense for this time to enjoy your life, relax, and let go. Simply be.

Full moon mini altar
Add blue candles, amethyst, bergamot essential oil, and sandalwood incense for this phase of maximum healing and transformation. Seeds planted in the new moon will now come into fruition.

Ghostbusting Potion

To rid a house of haunting intrusion, brew a peppermint-and-clove infusion. Draw fresh water and boil it in your teakettle. Place three cloves in the bottom of a teacup and add either a peppermint teabag or a handful of fresh mint leaves from your herb pots. Pour hot water into the cup and let it steep for 10 minutes, then let cool. Dip your fingers in the cup and sprinkle the potion throughout the space, and out the ghost will race. Burning frankincense and myrrh incense sends negative spirits flying away, as well.

TIMING: This ritual is best done during a waning moon.

New Moon, New Home

The new moon is the best possible time to make big changes, start a new project, or do a deep clean and energetic shift of your home. First, clean your home from top to bottom, and wash bed linen, towels, rugs, and tablecloths. Sweep and wash floors, recycle old newspapers, sort through those piles of paper on your desk, and get rid of things you don't need to keep; file everything else. Gather toys and games and put them in baskets for easy storage. Once your entire home is clean, decluttered, and lemony fresh, take the next step of the new moon ritual with a gathering of your fellow pagans. Ask each guest to bring food to share, and a small token to bless your home—crystals, flowers, seashells, candles, and other suitable altar offerings.

Gather together

- saucer of sea salt
- sage for smudging
- 1 white candle and 1 blue candle
- blue bowl filled with fresh water
- lavender incense
- lemon essential oil
- rose essential oil

Greet your guests and ask them to help you by smudging each room with the salt, sage, candle flames, sprinkles of water, and incense, while intoning the words opposite.

By the power of water,

Through the cleansing breath of air,

With the purifying heat of fire,

And the grounding energy of earth

We cleanse this space.

As you pass from room to room, anoint each door and windowsill
with the oil to prevent anything negative from crossing into the home.
Say this prayer to the goddess:

May the goddess bless this house,

Making it sacred and safe,

So that nothing but love and happiness

Shall enter through this door.

Finally, once you've gone through the house,
ask each guest to deposit their blessing token
on your altar. Gather around the table, dig into
the potluck dishes, and pour hearty glasses of
ale, wine, or mead. Give thanks for the
abundance of blessings and enjoy a feast
with your tribe.

Floral Fortification: Vesta's Hearth Offering

The sign of Cancer is very much oriented toward the love of home and family as well as security. Mixed dried flowers, otherwise known as potpourri, are now a popular household staple. It was a medieval custom to have them in the house, revived by the Victorians. Use different combinations for desired magical results; they help create a sacred sanctuary space.

Gather together

- 1 cup (20 g) of dried rose petals
- 1 cup (20 g) of dried marigold
- 1 cup (20 g) of dried lily petals
- basket or bowl for the flower blend
- clove essential oil
- cinnamon essential oil

TIMING: Either sun or moon in Cancer is a perfect time for this offering to the goddess of happy homes.

Put all the dried posies in the basket or bowl and sprinkle them with the essential oils. Place the mixture on the south point of your altar for the duration of a moon cycle. The sweet and spicy scent of the potpourri will spread a positive and protective energy to your home and your magical workings. A wreath of these same flowers with garlic cloves added will protect you from harm and illness. If you are a working witch, a small, sweet-smelling bowl of potpourri on your desk will provide constant comfort. If you have a fireplace, keep some on the mantle as an offering to the domestic goddess Vesta, she who keeps the home fire burning. When the scent has faded, burn it in your cast iron cauldron or a fireplace as an offering to her. Speak this invocation when making the offering:

Vesta, goddess of home and hearth,

Stand guard over this place I love.

Keep safe the ones I love.

This night, we breathe in peace.

These flowers are my offering to you.

So mote it be.

Lunar Lemon Power

Lemons contain the energy of the moon and the element of water. They can even be used to honor lunar deities. For millennia, people have used lemon oil in washing water for clothes and linens or cleaned their homes using hot water containing lemon leaves. The versatility of this beloved yellow fruit is fantastic. Instead of discarding lemon halves after you've used the juice for cooking or for making lemonade, save them to use around the home. This citrus fruit is a natural lightening agent that you can use in place of bleach (which should be used sparingly, if at all). And did you know that it can also perk up limp lettuce and kill weeds in the garden?

Cleaning cheese graters

Cut a lemon in half and run it over the grater. The acid in the lemon will help to break down the fat in the cheese. If the food is really stuck on the grater, dip the lemon in table salt and the salt will act as a scrubber; combined with the lemon, it will remove most foods.

Sanitizing metal jewelry

The acid in lemon juice also removes tarnish. Use just ¼ cup (60 ml) freshly squeezed lemon juice to 1½ cups (335 ml) water. You can also dip your silver into a glass of fizzy lemon soda (lemonade) and it will come out sparkling. However, don't use this combination on gold or pearls.

Preserving meat and cleaning your cutting board

Lemon juice creates an acidic environment, and bacteria need an alkaline environment to survive, so adding lemon to meat, fresh produce, and even water inhibits bacterial growth. A handy antibacterial and natural way to clean your cutting board after cooking meat is to rub lemon juice on it and let it sit overnight, before rinsing it in the morning. The lemon juice will kill bacteria and leave your board smelling fresh.

Restoring furniture and wood floors

Mix equal parts mayonnaise, olive oil, and lemon juice, and rub into wood furniture. This mix will add oil to the wood, and the lemon juice will cut through any build-up of polish. For floors, mix a little fresh lemon juice with olive oil.

chapter 2

Magical Meals

Moon-inspired delights and witch's brews

Kitchens are where the magic happens! Preparing and sharing food can be ceremonial, be it on a Tuesday school night or during the festivals of the season. With kitchen witchery, a simple bowl of savory soup can be the equal of a Samhain feast; the ingredients, the astrological aspects, phases of the moon, words spoken, and your intention make it so. Empowered by the wisdom of the moon, cooking is a magical act, and serving your family and friends is to serve the gods.

Harvest Moon Herb Soup

After the September equinox signals the change of seasons from summer to fall, you should start making pots of this seasonal meal, which is a guaranteed crowd pleaser. This autumnal soup is just as pleasing to the cook as it can be a quick supper, leftovers for lunch, and easily frozen for meals on the go. It is simple and delicious. Refrigerate overnight and the flavors will "marry" together to intensify and become an even more savory supper to serve to loved ones on this harvest moon night.

Gather together

- 3 large leeks, thinly sliced
- ¼ cup (60 ml) virgin olive oil
- 2 fresh garlic cloves, chopped
- 8 cups (2 liters) water
- 1 butternut squash, peeled, seeded, and coarsely grated
- 1 carrot, thinly sliced
- 4 large floury potatoes, such as Idaho or Maris Piper, or sweet potatoes, peeled and cut into small, spoon-sized chunks
- ¼ cup (5 g) fresh sage, finely chopped
- ¼ cup (10 g) fresh chives, finely chopped
- salt and pepper
- ¼ teaspoon celery salt

Serves 8

TIMING: On the eve of the first full moon of fall, gather the ingredients and prepare.

In a large iron skillet or frying pan (preferably well-seasoned by use in your kitchen) fry the leeks in the olive oil until they become soft and translucent. Add in the chopped garlic and cook until it is also soft and wafting a wonderful scent into your kitchen. Transfer to a soup pot, oil and all, and add the water, heating to a boil. Add all the veggies and herbs and turn the heat down to a simmer for 45 minutes. Test the potatoes to see if they are soft enough—do this by mashing with a wooden spoon. If they are still a bit hard, simmer for another 5 minutes. Turn the heat down very low, then season with salt and pepper. Add the celery salt as the last element of the year's abundance.

Serve in clay, wooden, or ceramic bowls by the light of a brown or yellow candle. A chunk of homemade bread would be the ideal seasonal accompaniment.

Amazing Maize: Baked Corn Pudding

This treat truly represents autumnal abundance. Not many of us have enough real estate to grow our own corn (otherwise known as maize), but this recipe is so tasty that you may want to give up the front lawn and get a crop going so that you have the freshest possible corn. In winter, you can use frozen corn (thaw before using). If you don't have fresh chives to hand, use the green part of a few scallions (spring onions) instead.

TIMING: This is a wonderful dish to bring to a Harvest Moon Feast.

Gather together

- 3 cups (375 g) corn kernels (about 6 ears)
- ¼ cup (25 g) chopped fresh chives
- 1 tablespoon chopped fresh thyme
- ¾ teaspoon salt
- ¼ teaspoon freshly ground black pepper
- 1½ cups (335 ml) low-fat (semi-skimmed) milk
- 2 tablespoons cream cheese
- 1 large egg, lightly beaten
- oil, for greasing

Serves 6

Preheat the oven to 350°F/180°C/Gas 4 and combine the corn, chives, thyme, salt, and pepper in a medium bowl. In another medium bowl, mix the milk, cream cheese, and egg. Add the milk mixture to the corn mixture and stir well to combine. Pour into an 11 x 7 in. (28 x 18 cm) baking dish coated with oil. Bake for 55 minutes, or until the top of the pudding is golden brown.

Corn Moon Clan Pot

Here we have the best of both worlds in one pot. Kids will love this "a-maize-ing" dish—they will ask for seconds!

Gather together

- 2 cups (200 g) dry penne pasta
- 8 ounces (225 g) diced tomatoes
- 1 jar enchilada sauce, 8 ounces (225 g)
- 1½ cups (350 ml) water
- 2 cups (250 g) shredded, cooked chicken
- 1 can black beans
- 1 cup (175 g) fresh (or frozen) corn
- 2 tablespoons salsa
- 2 tablespoons hot sauce
- ½ cup (50 g) Cheddar cheese, grated
- basil, cilantro (coriander), chives, avocado, and sour cream

TIMING: It can be a nice meal to serve during the Corn Moon—the September moon—and ritual feasts involving growth and transformation. Corn is associated with self-sustainability and fecundity, both of people and of the land. Sharing this dish is a time to remember and be grateful for all we have sown and all we have reaped to acknowledge the continuing cycles of life.

In a large pan over high heat, combine the pasta, tomatoes, enchilada sauce, and water. Heat to a boil, then reduce the temperature to medium heat; add the chicken, black beans, corn, and salsa. If your family likes it extra hot, throw in some green peppers to turn the heat up a notch. Reduce the heat to low, cover, and let simmer for 20 minutes, or until the pasta is tender and cooked through. Top with the cheese and the herbs; place the lid on the pan. Let the cheese melt in for 5 minutes and serve up this global crowd pleaser in heaping bowls.

Savory Sweet Potato Mooncakes

Hearty and oh-so-healthy, these pancakes make for a marvelous full-moon meal. Sweet potatoes are truly beneficial to women's health and contain estrogen; these tubers are good for you inside and outside as they also give your skin a nice boost. But their main magic for everyone is that they are a vehicle for grounding. Anytime you feel spacey or out-of-sorts or distracted, this food will serve you well.

Gather together

- 2 large semi-baked sweet potatoes, peeled and grated
- 1 large carrot, grated
- 3 eggs
- ½ tablespoon dried rosemary
- ½ tablespoon dried sage
- ½ cup (120 ml) olive oil
- 1 cup (240 ml) organic natural yogurt
- fresh chives

Makes 8 mooncakes

Mix the potatoes and carrot in a large bowl. Beat the eggs and add to the veggie mixture and mix thoroughly. Grind the rosemary and sage to a very fine powder in your mortar and pestle. Add the herbs to the veggie mixture, plus salt and pepper to taste. Shape into round balls, enough for eight mooncakes. Warm the oil slowly in a skillet/frying pan until it is hot. Place the balls in the oil and flatten into rounds with a spatula. Cook through for 8 minutes on each side or until they are golden brown and beginning to crisp on both sides. Plate up and top with organic yogurt and chives. If you are feeling decadent, dollop on sour cream, too.

Moon Drop Savory Scones

Serve these piping hot and straight out of the oven; this is a batch of ten delicious biscuits (scones). Better still, they're drop biscuits, which means there's no need to roll and cut the dough. If you are having more than five folks over for supper, double up the ingredients. These Moon Drop biscuits are excellent for dipping into soup and stews.

Gather together

- 1 cup (125 g) all-purpose (plain) flour
- ¼ teaspoon baking soda (bicarbonate of soda)
- 1 teaspoon baking powder
- ¼ teaspoon salt
- 3 tablespoons (40 g) cold unsalted butter
- ⅔ cup (160 ml) buttermilk

Makes 10 biscuits

Preheat the oven to 450°F/230°C/gas mark 8. In a medium bowl, combine the flour, baking soda, baking powder, and salt. Whisk gently to blend the ingredients. With two knives, cut the butter in until the mixture looks like coarse meal. Add in the buttermilk and stir until it is blended, but do not over stir. Drop heaping tablespoons of the mixture onto an oiled baking sheet; you should separate the biscuits by 2 inches (5cm). Bake for 12 minutes and pull the biscuits out once they are a light-golden, buttery brown.

Home-Brewed Apple Cider Vinegar

Sometimes I think that I didn't so much choose my home but that the tree in the backyard chose me. We are true companions and I have learned much from my beloved tree, which is one of the few remaining from an apple orchard from the 1800s. It is truly goddess-blessed land, watched over by Pomona, the apple goddess. Every autumn is a bountiful harvest, letting nothing go to waste. After the best apples are used to make pies, anything left over is perfect for making apple cider and the accompanying vinegar. There are many devotees to apple cider vinegar as it is one of nature's most effective remedies; it is an antioxidant and excellent as an immune booster, for weight loss, and for abetting digestive issues, for starters.

Gather together

- 1 pound (500 g) apples, rinsed, chopped, organic, and pesticide-free
- 1-quart (1-liter) canning jar with sealable lid and ring, such as a Mason jar, clean and sterilized
- ¼ cup (50 g) sugar
- ½ quart (500 ml) freshly boiled water
- 2 coffee filters
- 2 clean rubber bands
- bowl

Fill the jar with the chopped apples, then add the sugar. Pour in the hot water to the very top of the canning jar. Cover the lid with the jar ring and a coffee filter secured by a rubber band. Store the jar out of direct sunlight but on a warm shelf—beside a refrigerator is a perfect spot and the slight warmth will speed up the fermentation process.

After just a few days, the apple mixture will begin to bubble and foam. After two weeks, strain the liquid into a bowl, clean the jar, then refill the jar with the strained liquid. Cover exactly as before using a coffee filter, canning jar ring, and rubber band. Store on the same warm shelf.

After another two weeks, the liquid will appear cloudy and a film will form on the surface which you should skim off. This is referred to as the "mother" and can be used as a starter for future cider vinegars. Just refrigerate and add a tablespoon of mother into a clean canning jar that has a cup of water in it.

Six weeks from the start, your fermentation process will be complete and the apple cider vinegar is ready to use. Apple cider vinegar can keep for two years and it is not necessary to store it in the refrigerator unless you prefer it chilled. You should be brewing up a batch of apple cider vinegar at least once a year and, over time, you will perfect yours.

Herbal Vinegar

If you love everything about lavender, you may well want to create your own lavender vinegar. Many herbs make for excellent vinegars, so pay attention to which ones are especially appealing to you as you go about your gardening. The more herbs you pack into the jar, the higher the mineral content in your vinegar, which makes it more flavorful and healthy.

Once you have your own apple cider vinegar or a premade organic kind you and your family love, pick an herb you know works for you and pack a quart canning jar as full as you can with it. Pour room-temperature apple cider vinegar to cover and seal with paper and bands and pop back on a dark corner shelf for six weeks, giving it a shake once a week.

At the end of the infusion period, strain out any remaining compostable twigs or stems that remain, if any, and store in a colored bottle and add a pretty label. These make wonderful gifts so I recommend you get a set of labels for all your witchy brews.

Herbal Infusion Invocation

For any witch, the kitchen is the laboratory for alchemy.
The transference of the pure essence of an herb into oil or liqueur is
nothing less than magic. Adding the following step to the process of
infusing honors its alchemical aspect and adds enchantment to the
final product. After you have bottled up your infusions, and before you
store them in a dark pantry, place them on your altar. Check your
almanac (see pages 62–65) to see what sign the sun and moon are in,
and what the moon phase is. Have a pretty label and a colored pen at
the ready.

Light a green candle, hold one of the bottles in both hands, and pray aloud:

Under this moon and sun,

Green magic binds into one.

By my hand, I filled this bottle with grace,

To bring enjoyment to all who come to this place.

Blessings for all; and so be it.

Take the pen and write on the label the kind of herbal oil you have made—for example:

APPLE BRANDY SPIRITS
*Made on June 15, under the Gemini Sun
and Taurus New Moon.*

Keep records of your results in your Book of Shadows.

Full Moon Tea

It amuses me to see how trendy cold-brewed tea has become as hedgewitches and wise women have been making this delightful concoction for centuries. It is made in the same way as Sun Tea, which is gently heated by the warmth of the sun but is brewed at night in the light of the moon.

Gather together

- 1-quart (1-liter) canning jar with lid
- cold, pure spring water
- 4 herbal teabags or 3 heaping tablespoons of dried herbs of your choice
- large tea ball or small muslin bag (if using dried herbs)

Fill the jar with the spring water and add the herbal teabags (or the tea ball/muslin bag filled with the dried herbs). Seal the lid on the canning jar and leave it outside or on your windowsill so it can be exposed to the light of the moon. When you awaken in the morning, you will have cold-brewed tea. Do make notes in your Book of Shadows for which brews taste best to you. I can tell you that when the full moon is in the signs of Taurus, Cancer, Virgo, Libra, or Pisces, the tea is most delicious to me, with my current favorites being ginger peach and cinnamon hibiscus.

HERBS FOR FULL MOON TEA

Here are a few suggestions for herbs and plants to use for your Full Moon Tea, as well as Sun Tea and traditional tea.

Beautiful blue borage

This sweetly blue flower has long been used to decorate cakes and other sweets, but also has a light and pleasant flavor that makes for a lovely, fruity tea. You might want to grow borage in your garden because it attracts pollinators such as bees. Borage tea is very calming and is a marvelous anti-inflammatory.

Delicious dandelion

The gardener's bane should actually be greeted gladly, as these humble yellow weeds are superfoods! They make a hearty and healthy tea, and are excellent as salad greens, so you can take advantage of all the nutrients. If that was not enough, dandelions can also be used to make excellent wine!

Helpful hyssop

Both the beautiful purple flowers of hyssop and its leaves have a tangy licorice flavor. This true medicinal can be used from stem to leaf to flower for brewing soothing teas to relieve pain, quiet respiratory complaints, and support your digestion.

Noble nasturtiums

These are one of my favorites, because anyone can grow them anywhere. They reseed themselves, so you only need to plant them once and you will have a salad green, a spicy tea, and gorgeous flowers that cheer you up every time you see them. The leaves of the sun-colored flower can be dried and brewed in a tea that is packed with vitamin C and is capable of both healing and preventing colds and flu.

Loveliest lavender

So versatile, this herb is an absolute necessity in healing magic. While it is nearly universally used as an oil, lotion, and aromatic, it is often forgotten that it makes for a terrific tea. Add bergamot and you will get both an energy boost and a sense of calm. In this case, just breathing in the scent of lavender tea will bring serenity and wellbeing.

Radiant rose

I have an old-fashioned rose with gorgeous orange blossoms that has a tangy scent that is spectacular. Flavors vary depending on the variety and growing conditions, so petals can be both spicy and sweet, but in general darker petals have more flavor. Brewed into a tea and sweetened with honey, rose will attract love into your life and a sense of self-love as well. The scent and energy of rose is very gentle and will raise your vibration and uplift your personal energy.

Vivid violet

This tea might be the most unusual of all, as it has an enchanted color and can be used to brew a lovely blue-green tea that helps with pain relief, insomnia, and coughs. Johnny jump-ups and their cousin pansy can be used as well. Utterly charming and good for you, too!

Jasmine Joy Ritual

Jasmine tea is a delightful concoction and can create an aura of bliss and conviviality. It is available at any grocer or purveyor of organic goods, but homegrown is even better. Brew a cup of jasmine tea and let it cool. Add two parts lemonade to one part jasmine tea and drink the mixture with a good friend. Jasmine is a vine and represents the intertwining of people. You will be more bonded to anyone with whom you share this sweet ritual. This is also a tonic that you can indulge in when alone.

TIMING: I recommend brewing up a batch every Monday, or "Moon Day," to ensure that each week is filled with joyfulness.

As the jasmine tea steeps, pray:

On this Moon Day in this new week,

I call upon the spirits to guide joy to my door.

By this moon on this day, I call upon Selene,
goddess fair

To show me the best way to live.

For this, I am grateful.

Blessed be the brew; blessed be me.

Telepathy Tea

The humble dandelion, abhorred by lawn keepers everywhere, hides its might very well. Dandelion root tea can call upon the spirit of anyone whose advice you might need.

Simply place a freshly brewed simple using this herbal root on your bedroom altar or nightstand. Before you sleep, say the name of your helper aloud seven times. In a dream or vision, the spirit will visit you and answer all your questions.

During medieval times, this spell was used to find hidden treasure. Chaucer, who was well-versed in astrology and other metaphysics, also advised this tried-and-true tea.

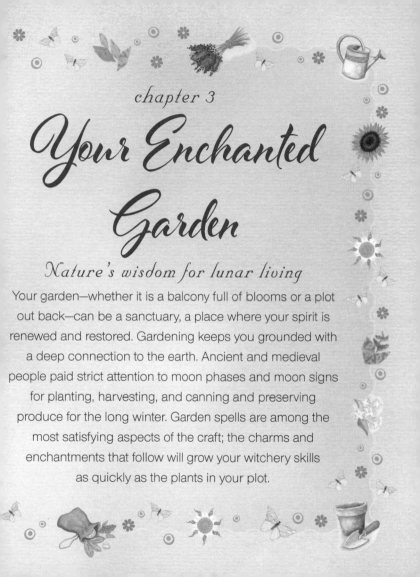

chapter 3

Your Enchanted Garden

Nature's wisdom for lunar living

Your garden—whether it is a balcony full of blooms or a plot out back—can be a sanctuary, a place where your spirit is renewed and restored. Gardening keeps you grounded with a deep connection to the earth. Ancient and medieval people paid strict attention to moon phases and moon signs for planting, harvesting, and canning and preserving produce for the long winter. Garden spells are among the most satisfying aspects of the craft; the charms and enchantments that follow will grow your witchery skills as quickly as the plants in your plot.

Your Magical Intent

Do you use chamomile regularly? Do you purify your space with sage? Are rosemary, mint, and lavender favorites in your sachets and teas? Think of all the herbs and plants you love and use often, then begin researching their upkeep and care. Make sure to research your planting zone so you get the optimal climate to nurture your plants and herbs. Once you have planned your plantings, infuse your plot with magical intention. Keep careful track of your progress in your Book of Shadows. As you grow in experience and expertise, so will the healing power of your plot.

Remember to research plants and herbs that can be toxic or poisonous to ensure the safety of children or our canine and feline friends. Many a beloved power flower handed down to us is excellent for magical workings but not at all appropriate for tea, edibles, or such things. Make sure visiting children stay far away from wisteria, rhododendron, lily of the valley, narcissus, foxglove, larkspur, hydrangea, and oleander. They are beautiful but deadly, literally.

Every new moon is an opportunity to sow seeds for new beginnings and deepen your magical intent. Your plantings can be a tool you use for a better life, bringing brighter health and greater abundance, as well as mindfulness and serenity. Nature is our greatest teacher and a garden is a gift through which you both give and receive.

New Moon: Sowing the Seeds of Positive Change

Nature is the ultimate healer. The new moon is the time to plant seeds for the change you desire. If you want more calmness and less stress, sow the seeds for that. Go to the nursery or hardware store and buy seeds for a serenity garden: lavender, thyme, mint, chamomile.

TIMING: You can do this on a new moon at any time of year if you plant the seeds in herb pots on your windowsill. If the weather is warm and you have an outdoor space, plant them there and make that your outdoor serenity space.

After you have planted your herb seeds, pray aloud:

As these seeds grow,

More tranquility will flow.

Healing Mother Earth and Sister Moon,

I turn to you to bring calm and serenity soon,

Under this new moon and in this old earth.

So mote it be. Blessed be to all.

Gently water your new-moon garden, and affirmative change
will begin that very day.

Wish Upon a Waxing Moon

Sanctify your garden space and transform an ivy plant into a botanical "familiar" with this spell and an outdoor altar.

TIMING: Perform this spell when the moon is waxing, growing larger toward the phase of fullness.

Gather green and purple candles and anoint them with sandalwood and rose oil, respectively. Place the candles on a large, flat rock or your garden wall to create a simple outdoor altar. Place a small, potted ivy vine on the altar, along with a cup of water. Burn sandalwood incense on the northern side of your outdoor altar. Now close your eyes and meditate upon your hopes and dreams of growth—personal, business, spiritual, for loved ones.

When the incense has almost completely burned, take the ivy and plant it in the optimal spot in your garden, where it can thrive and spread, creating beauty as it vines on a wall or fence. Use the cup to water the plant.

Now bow and pray, using the words below.

As this living thing expands,

So shall the power of this magical space grow.

Oh, goddess of the Earth, I dedicate my magic to you.

Harm to none and only good work from this holy space.

Now, as the ivy flourishes, so will you. Continually revitalize your
outdoor altar by adorning it with sacred objects that have meaning
to you: iridescent feathers, a lovely rock, a bright red pomegranate,
a beautiful white rose, or anything else you find in nature
that will make a perfect offering.

Basil and Mint Money Bag

Rather than chasing money or possessions, you can simply draw them toward you with wisdom from days gone by. Fill a tiny green pouch with the herbs basil and mint, three cinnamon sticks, one silver dollar (or a shiny pound coin), and a green stone—peridot or a smooth, mossy-colored pebble of jade would be perfect. The untrained eye might perceive this as a bag of weeds and rocks but any kitchen witch recognizes this is a powerful tool for creating dynamic change in your life and attracting good fortune.

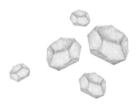

TIMING: Prepare your attraction pouch during a waxing moon; the strongest power would be when the sun or moon is in Taurus, Cancer, or Capricorn.

Hold the pouch over frankincense incense and, as the smoke blesses the bag, say:

The moon is a silver coin; this I know.

I carry lunar magic with me everywhere I go.

Blessings upon thee and me as my abundance grows.

Carry this power pouch with you as you go about your day—to work, to the store, on your daily walks, to social events. Soon, blessings will shower down upon you. You might even receive a gift or literally find money in your path.

Planting Newness into Your Life

From a nearby gardening or hardware store, get an assortment of seed packets to plant newness into your life. If your thumb is not the greenest, try nasturtiums, which are extremely hardy, grow quickly, and spread, beautifying any area. They also re-seed themselves.

TIMING: Plant your new seeds on a new-moon morning.

Draw a square in your yard with a "found-in-nature" wand—a fallen branch. Apartment dwellers can use a planter on the deck or a big pot for this ritual. Each corner of the square needs a candle and a special stone. Mark the corners in a clockwise fashion as follows:

- Green candle and peridot or jade for creativity, prosperity, and growth.

- Orange candle and jasper or onyx for clear thinking and highest consciousness.

- Blue candle and turquoise or celestine for serenity, kindness, and a happy heart.

- White candle and quartz or limestone for purification and safety.

Repeat this chant as you light each candle:

Greatest Gaia, I turn to you to help me renew.

Under this new moon and in this old earth.

Blessings to you; blessings to me. Blessed be.

Put the seeds under the soil with your fingers and tamp them down gently with your wand—the branch—which you should also stick in the ground at this time. Water your new-moon garden and affirmative change will begin in your life that very day.

Lunar Almanac: Moon Signs of The Times

The astrological signs of the moon are of great significance. Each moon sign has a special meaning that has been passed down through the centuries. Ancient and medieval people paid strict attention to moon phases and moon signs for planting, harvesting, and canning and preserving produce for the long winter. Here is a guide to each sign, with tried-and-true lore from olden days along with applications for today's rituals.

ARIES is a barren and dry sign that is perfect for planting, weeding, haying, and harvesting. Moon in Aries is the optimum time for beginning a big project, such as digging a garden plot for the first time or starting an herb garden in your kitchen.

TAURUS is an earthy, moist sign that is excellent for planting root crops such as potatoes, beets, and peanuts. Moon in Taurus is a good time for buying a garden plot or farm, or investing in your home. It is also the best time for planting leafy vegetables, such as lettuce, spinach, and cabbage.

GEMINI is another dry sign that is the best time for mowing, cutting, and getting rid of weeds or pests. Melon seeds thrive if they are planted now. Since communication is at a peak during Gemini Moon, it is also a great time for a garden party!

CANCER is a fruitful watery sign that is conducive to planting; in fact, it is the most productive sign of all. Hearth and home are the focus now, and Moon in Cancer is a good time for lunar rituals.

LEO is the driest and least fertile of all moon signs, good only for cutting and mowing. Leo Moon is good for weeding and removing "volunteers," such as thorny brambles, that sprout uninvited.

VIRGO is both damp and barren, but a great time for cultivation. Virgo Moon is good for hard work and major projects. This moon sign is the perfect time for all kinds of healing spell work and for making tinctures, tonics, floral waters, and essences.

LIBRA is both wet and fruitful, and is wonderful for grains, vines, root crops, and flowers. This is the time to beautify your home and garden and add refinement to your sacred space. Moon in Libra is the most favorable time for working with fragrant flowers, vines, and shrubs.

SCORPIO, humid and bountiful, is good for all types of planting. This is an especially good time to work with fruit trees, including grafting. Tomatoes are best transplanted during Scorpio Moon.

SAGITTARIUS is another fire sign that is a poor time for planting and is best-spent harvesting and storing. It is an excellent time for working and improving the soil, and good for reaping root crops.

CAPRICORN is an earth sign that is also wet, and is excellent for grafting, pruning, and planting trees and shrubs. It is also an ideal time for planting root crops. Rituals relating to future plans and visioning can be started now, and trees can be saved and healed.

AQUARIUS is an infertile and parched moon time that is best for harvesting, weeding, and dispelling pests. The Aquarian Moon is very good for storing, canning, and preserving. Onions thrive when planted during this sign.

PISCES is fecund and fruitful and is good for all kinds of planting. It is remarkable for fruit of all kinds. The highly sensitive Moon in Pisces is great for spells and charms.

May Magic:
Flower Moon Invocation

The fullest phase of the moon can be the time for the greatest of magic—you can conjure your heart's desire and tackle the "big things" of life, whether that be a problem to resolve, a major life transition, such as seeking a new job or home, whatever your truest wish. This gorgeous spring Flower Moon provides an optimal opportunity to strive for the new, to initiate a phase of transformation in your life that will last long after the full moon has waxed into darkness.

TIMING: Start this invocation when the full moon of May reaches the highest point in the night sky.

Gather red and green apples, candles of the same colors, a few grains of seed corn from a gardening store or natural grocery, along with three stalks of lavender and a long strand of night-blooming jasmine. Leave these offerings on your altar all day.

Light one red and one green candle on your kitchen altar. Wind the jasmine and lavender into a crown for the top of your head, breathing in the lovely scent the flowers produce. For three minutes, visualize your desired change for this spell. Holding an apple in each hand, speak the words of the spell on the left while circling the candlelit altar clockwise three times.

Eat from both apples until you are fully satisfied, then bury the corn seeds and the cores near your kitchen door or the rightmost corner of your garden. With the spring rains, your intentions will come into being. By the fall full moon, you will be harvesting the bounty of change from this spell, with great gratitude.

Through the power of Earth and Air, Water and Fire.

As I bite this fruit of knowledge,

I am thus inspired.

All possibilities are before me. And so it is.

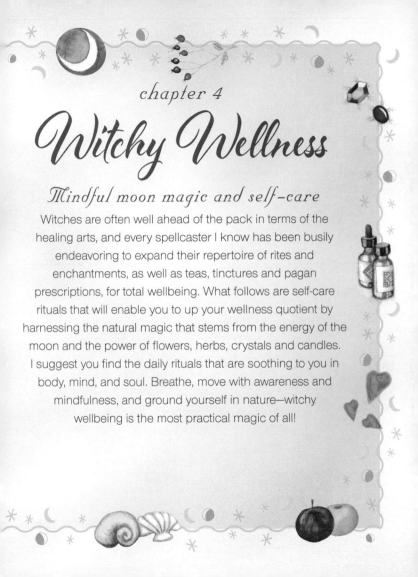

Witchy Wellness

Mindful moon magic and self-care

Witches are often well ahead of the pack in terms of the healing arts, and every spellcaster I know has been busily endeavoring to expand their repertoire of rites and enchantments, as well as teas, tinctures and pagan prescriptions, for total wellbeing. What follows are self-care rituals that will enable you to up your wellness quotient by harnessing the natural magic that stems from the energy of the moon and the power of flowers, herbs, crystals and candles. I suggest you find the daily rituals that are soothing to you in body, mind, and soul. Breathe, move with awareness and mindfulness, and ground yourself in nature—witchy wellbeing is the most practical magic of all!

The Goddess of Healing: Artemis Invocation

Creating a healing altar will safeguard your physical health and that of your loved ones. Your altar is your sacred workspace. It is charged with your personal power. Set up your healing altar facing north, the direction associated with the energy of manifestation. Your shrine to the healing craft should be highly personal and represent all that signifies wellness to you. This altar is dedicated to Artemis, goddess of the healing moon (see page 72).

TIMING: Set up the altar at midnight. North is the direction of the hour of midnight, the "witching hour," and an altar set up facing north at midnight promises potent magic.

Gather together

- white fabric
- 2 green candles, for health, in green glass holders or votive glasses
- a small statue of Artemis, or a moon-shaped symbol to represent her
- incense such as sandalwood, camphor, or frankincense
- healing crystals and objects that bring comfort

To ensure healthful beginnings, drape the white fabric over your altar to make a tabula rasa, or altar equivalent to a blank slate. Take the candles and position them in the two farthest corners of the altar. Place the Artemis statue at the center of the altar. Place an incense burner between the two candles and light the incense.

Now adorn your altar with objects that symbolize healing energy to you. You may perhaps choose a candleholder carved from a chunk of amethyst crystal, which contains healing properties; an abalone shell with the iridescent magic of the oceans; a sweet-smelling bundle of sage; a small citrus plant bursting with the restorative power of vitamins; or a bowl of curative salts from the sea.

These symbolic items, and any others that you select, will energize your altar with the magic that lives inside you. It is also important that the altar be pleasing to your eye and makes you feel good when you look at it so that you want to spend time there each and every day. After you have been performing rituals there for a while, a positive healing energy field will radiate from your altar.

Artemis, Goddess of the Healing Moon

Artemis is one of the best-known goddesses and, as it turns out, is one of the most needed as she is a healing divinity. She is the Greek goddess of the moon. In her Roman form, Diana, she is the deity to whom Dianic witches and priestesses are devoted. She is a bringer of luck, the goddess of the hunt, and a powerful deity for magic and spellwork. As the huntress, she can help you search out anything you are looking for, whether it is tangible or intangible. As a lunar deity, she can illuminate you. Invoke Artemis when you want to practice moon magic, by saying aloud "I call upon you, beloved Artemis." I suggest you study her mythology further to design original lunar ceremonies. Enshrine her by dedicating an altar or sacred space to her to bring about any of her marvelous qualities and to bring about healing.

Contentment Ritual

You can create a week of blissful and composed calm by casting the following spell on a waning moon Monday.

Gather together

- purple candle
- hibiscus or violet essential oil
- bouquet of purple flowers (violets, for example)

TIMING: On a Monday, as the moon grows smaller in the sky, try this spell.

Anoint your purple candle with the essential oil. Place the candle on your altar beside a vase of fresh violets or other purple flowers. Sit in front of your altar as twilight begins, and when the sun is completely gone, light the candle and chant:

Any care and despair begone.

Here with the mountain, the river, the tree, the grass, and the moon.

I receive my strength from Nature and she is my center.

Tomorrow and the next, all gladness will enter.

Harm to none, only good.

A Spell to Quell Anxiety

With this spell, you can quiet any worries that may be keeping you awake at night. When our moon ebbs, another grows forth, and so it goes for our creativity and renewal cycles.

Gather together

- 1 vanilla bean pod
- sandalwood incense
- amber resin
- charcoal cake for burning incense
- fireproof glass or clay dish
- 1 black or gray candle

TIMING: As the sun sets on a waning moon day, cast this spell.

Set aside a small piece of the vanilla bean, then grind together a teaspoon each of sandalwood, amber, and the remainder of the vanilla bean using either the back of a spoon or your mortar and pestle. Burn this resin-based mixture on a piece of charcoal in the fireproof dish on your altar. Light the black or gray candle, for protection. Rub the reserved small piece of vanilla bean in your palm until the scent begins to waft up thanks to the heat in your hands. Concentrate on the flame and rub the same vanilla essence on your temples and place your hand over your heart.

Begin to meditate:

Sometimes I doubt myself...

Sometimes I worry needlessly...

From now on, I will trust my innate wisdom and instincts.

All anxiety is leaving my mind and body.

Thank you la lune, goddess of the moon.

Blessed be.

Blow out the candle and throw it into a fireplace or your cast iron cauldron to burn away. You must completely destroy the candle because it contains the energy of your anxiety and fear.
Now, go and worry no more.

Lunar Elixir: Restorative Full Moon Infusion

The full moon is a truly auspicious time and one to savor and make the most of. Try this restorative Lunar Elixir anytime your energy level is low to bolster mind, body, and spirit.

Gather together

- 1 teaspoon sliced fresh ginger root
- 1 teaspoon jasmine tea leaves
- 1 teaspoon peppermint tea leaves
- 2 cups (480 ml) fresh water
- a teapot and a mug

TIMING: Full moon phases last two days, so make this elixir on the first night at midnight.

Just before midnight, brew and strain an infusion of these healthful and energizing herbs. Once it is cool, pour it into your favorite mug and relish the aromatic steam for a moment. Wait for the stroke of midnight. Now, step outside and drink the elixir during this enchanted hour in the glow of moonlight. You will immediately feel clearer, more centered, and more focused.

Quick Tip: MOON SPELL SECRETS

In late spring and early summer, you will see a shape resembling a dragon on the moon—an auspicious time for new beginnings, business, and magic related to work and money. The moon dragon is visible when Jupiter occupies the center of the sky. Ventures begun under its influence will meet with great success.

Awaken the Imagination: Age of Aquarius Spell

Often, our state of mind grows restless when life becomes too routine. Inspiration and imagination will remedy this instantly.

Gather together:

- 1 green candle
- 1 yellow candle
- an amethyst crystal
- a green apple
- a small pine branch

TIMING: Check your favorite celestial calendar to plan this spell for when the moon is in the sign of brilliance, Aquarius.

At one hour before midnight, place the two candles on your altar. Next to them, place the crystal, apple, and pine branch. At 11:11 pm, hold the apple in the palm of your right hand and, while circling the candlelit altar clockwise four times, speak the spell on the opposite page.

Sun and moon, awaken me tonight

With the power of Earth and Air, Fire and Water.

As I bite this fruit of knowledge, I am inspired.

All possibilities are before me. And so it is.

Eat the apple, then bury the seeds in your garden or in a potted plant. You will walk on a path new with promise of anything you can imagine. Keep the crystal and pine on your altar for as long as you wish and they will spark inspiration every time you see them.

Crown Chakra Tonic
for Insight

This magical hair tonic will clear your mind, awaken your senses, and open your crown chakra (the energy point at the top of your head), preparing the way for telepathic insight.

Gather together

- 2-ounce (55-ml) squeeze bottle
- 4 drops rosewood essential oil
- 2 tablespoons rosemary essential oil
- a palmful of plain unscented hair conditioner

TIMING: Ideally, perform this ritual when the sun or moon is in the truth-seeking signs of Gemini or Sagittarius for the greatest effect.

Combine the oils and conditioner in the bottle. Shake well and pour onto your freshly shampooed hair while singing:

Sweetness, born of Rose,

Fly me on the wings of dreams.

We are made of sacred earth, purest water,

Sacred fire, wildest wind.

Blessing upon me. Blessing upon thee.

So mote it be.

At the very least, you will have visions and great clarity. You might even realize your true destiny. Wear your new wisdom gloriously, like a crown.

Encouragement Spell: Quell Negative Self-Talk

This spell helps you subdue the inner voices of negativity and inner criticism that get in the way of simple joy.

Gather together

- 1 teaspoon patchouli resin
- 1 teaspoon rose hips
- vanilla bean
- charcoal wafer
- fireproof dish or incense burner
- incense bowl
- gray candle

TIMING: Perform this spell as the sun sets on a waning moon day.

Grind together the patchouli resin, rose hips, and the whole vanilla bean. Burn this mixture on the charcoal in the incense bowl on your altar. Light a gray candle (for protection) and meditate on the flame. As you meditate, think about whether you sometimes doubt yourself and your instincts. Visualize clearing that from your mind.

Think about your talents and your
potential as you chant:

La lune, Goddess of the Moon,

As you may grow, so do I.

Here, tonight, under your darkest light,

I shall embrace all within me that is good and right,

And bid goodbye to all the rest. Blessed be.

Blow out the candle and cast it into a fireplace, an outdoor firepot, or
wherever it can be melted down completely and safely. You must
completely destroy the candle, as it contains the energy of your inner
critic. You should feel lighter and brighter almost immediately!

Ancient Secrets to Radiance

To strengthen your vivacity and vitality and prompt the highest of spirits, this incense enhanced with essential oils will do it.

Gather together

- 1 teaspoon myrrh incense
- 1 teaspoon sandalwood incense
- 1 teaspoon frankincense incense
- mortar and pestle
- 3 drops sandalwood essential oil
- 3 drops frankincense essential oil
- 3 drops amber essential oil
- fireproof dish and charcoal wafer

TIMING: This incense brings forth the greatest result if burned during the full moon phase.

Start by grinding all the incense in your mortar and pestle until they are mixed together. Add the essential oils and grind again lightly. Cover the charcoal wafer in your fireproof dish with the mixture and light the incense. Silently speak the following spell:

Under this moon in this night,

With every word, I draw down delight.

With every breath, I feel the light.

Tonight, this moon grows more bright.

Tonight, I embrace life with all my might,

So mote it be.

Let the incense burn for as long as you wish.

Recharging Weekend Wonder: Natural Remedy Potion

This natural remedy is an excellent way to refresh after a hectic week.

Gather together

- 2 drops rosemary essential oil
- 3 drops bergamot essential oil
- 2 drops jasmine essential oil
- 3 drops lavender essential oil
- 6 drops carrier oil
- a small ceramic or glass bowl

TIMING: This tincture is most potent right after the sun sets, by the light of the waxing or full moon.

Blend the essential oils and carrier oil in the bowl. Take off your shoes so you can be more grounded. Walk outside, stand on your deck or by an open window.

Now, close your eyes, lift your head to the moon, and recite aloud:

Bright moon goddess, eternal and wise,

Give your strength to me now.

As I breathe, you are alive in me for this night.

Health to all, calm to me.

So mote it be.

Gently rub one drop of Natural Remedy Potion on each pulse point:
both wrists, behind your ear lobes, on the base of your neck, and
behind your knees. As the oil surrounds you with its warm scent,
you will be filled with a quiet strength.

Respite Rite: A Good Night's Sleep Herbs

The sweet scent of petals and herbs can bring deep rest when you cast this spell.

Gather together

- ½ cup (½ oz/15 g) fresh white and pink rose petals
- ⅓ cup (½ oz/15 g) dried woolly thyme
- pinch of ground cinnamon
- 1 vanilla bean
- small, lidded box
- white paper and pen
- white quartz crystal

TIMING: Try to perform this spell during a full moon.

Mix the flowers and herbs together and use some to fill the bottom
half of the box. Chop the vanilla bean with your bolline and add to
the box. Now write down five qualities you wish for in regard to rest
and rejuvenation. For example, when I did this a few years ago,
I wrote that I wanted to get up an hour earlier each day feeling fresh
and ready for the world. Sure enough, I was able to do that after one
week. This manifesting magic works! Fold the paper at least once,
to fit into the box. Fill up the box with the rest of the flowers and
herbs mix. Nestle the crystal in the herbs right at the top and close
the lid. Each night, open the box and take a sniff to remind yourself
of your search for true restoration.

Shekinah's Garden of Eden Salts

Shekinah translates to "She who dwells within" and is the Hebrew name for the female aspect of God. Olden legend has it that she co-created the world side by side with Yahweh, the god of Israel. This simple recipe recalls the scents and primal memories of that Edenic paradise.

Gather together

- 3 cups (385 g) Epsom salts
- ½ cup (120 ml) sweet almond oil
- 1 tablespoon glycerin
- 4 drops ylang-ylang essential oil
- 2 drops jasmine essential oil

TIMING: The ideal time to use this scrub is during a waxing morning moon or at midnight during a new moon.

Mix well and store in a colored and well-capped glass bottle. Prepare for the ritual rub by lighting citrus- and rose-scented candles. Step out of your clothes and hold the salts in the palms of your hand. Pray aloud using the words opposite.

Shekinah, may your wisdom guide me,
My body is a temple to you.
Here I worship today, with heart and hands,
Body and soul.
I call upon you for healing,
Shekinah, bring me breath and life.
Ancient one, I thank you
With heart and hands,
Body and soul.

Use these salts with a clean washcloth or new sponge and gently scrub your body while standing. You will glow with health and inner peace.

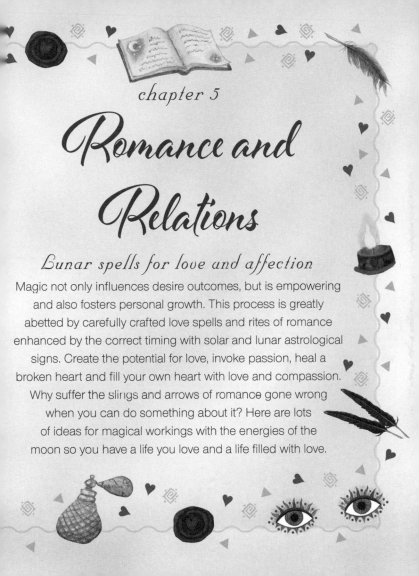

chapter 5

Romance and Relations

Lunar spells for love and affection

Magic not only influences desire outcomes, but is empowering and also fosters personal growth. This process is greatly abetted by carefully crafted love spells and rites of romance enhanced by the correct timing with solar and lunar astrological signs. Create the potential for love, invoke passion, heal a broken heart and fill your own heart with love and compassion. Why suffer the slings and arrows of romance gone wrong when you can do something about it? Here are lots of ideas for magical workings with the energies of the moon so you have a life you love and a life filled with love.

New Moon, New Friends

When I moved to San Francisco, I didn't know a soul, but I used this tried-and-tested trick to fill my life with friends.

Gather together

- 1 candle of any color or size
- your favorite incense

TIMING: Try this on a new moon Friday (Freya's Day, which is ruled by Venus, is ideal for fun, love, flirtation, gossip, and good times).

Light the candle and incense. Breath in the sacred smoke and dance around, arms held upward, joyously. Say aloud the words of the spell opposite.

I call upon you, friend Freya,
To fill my life with love and joy. I call upon you, Goddess,
To bring unto me that which I enjoy
In the form of people, wise and kind.
This I ask and give thanks for, blessed be.

This resulted in me having friends who have stuck with me through thick and thin; I can count on them for boundless love and they bring so much joy to my life.

First Moon of New Love: Candle Bell Spell

Try this spell if you are in a phase of your life where you wish to attract new love.

Gather together

- 1 pink votive candle
- a tray
- 1 long-stemmed red rose bud
- a small hand bell
- rose essential oil

TIMING: Begin this Candle Bell Spell on the first night of the full moon.

Check your lunar almanac and on the first night of the full moon, place the candle on the tray on your altar. Lay the rose bud and bell beside the candle. Anoint the candle with the rose essential oil. For the next two nights, cup the candle in your hands and direct loving thoughts into its flame for at least 5 minutes.

On the last night of the full moon, take a thorn from the rose and carve the name of your heart's desire into the candle wax, reciting:

I will find true love.

Light the candle and ring the bell thrice, saying:

As this candle begins to burn, a lover true will I earn.

As this flame burns ever higher,

I will feel my lover's fire.

Ring the bell three more times and allow the candle to burn for a few minutes while gazing at the flame. Keep notes in your bedside journal or your Book of Shadows and note how long it takes for true love to walk into your life. It will be interesting to look back and see where it happens, what sign the moon and sun are in, and all the details that will inform your future magical workings.

Very Berry Enchantment Ink

In the days of yore, people often made their own inks, thus imbuing them with a deeply personal energy. They simply went to the side of the road and gathered blackberries from the vines that grew there. Often, a bird flying overhead will supply a gift of volunteer vines, best cultivated by a fence where it can climb, making berry picking easier. When it comes to matters of the heart, contracts, legal letters, and any document of real importance that you feel the need to make your mark upon, an artfully made ink can help you do just that; it can also help you write unforgettable love letters and memorable memorandums.

Gather together

- ⅛ cup (40 ml) crushed berry juice
- 9 drops of burgundy wine
- dark red ink
- small metal bowl
- apple essential oil
- vial or small, sealable bottle
- paper and envelope
- feather
- red candle

TIMING: This spell is best performed during the waning moon.

Mix the juice, wine, and red ink in a small, metal bowl. Carefully pour it into the vial and add one drop of the apple essence. Seal the bottle and shake gently.

Incant aloud the spell below:

By my hand, this spell is wrought.

With this ink, I will author my own destiny.

And have the happy life and love I sought.

So mote it be.

Now write the fate you envision for yourself in the near and far future, using the enchantment ink and a feather for a pen. Let it dry and seal it in an envelope and keep it on your altar until the new moon phase. Then, by the light of a red candle, open the letter to yourself and read it aloud. Afterwards, burn the paper, using the candle, and scatter the ashes in your garden. By the next new moon, you will begin to reap the results of the positive plans you invoked.

Oil of Love

Indulge in this sensually satisfying ritual concoction that will make your skin glow and will also surround you with a seductive aura. Your personal vibration will draw people toward you thanks to this lovely essence.

Gather together

- 2 tablespoons (30 ml) sweet almond carrier (or base) oil
- 6 drops jasmine essential oil
- 6 drops rose essential oil
- 1 ounce (30 g) aloe vera gel
- 3-ounce (85 ml) squeeze bottle
- 1 tablespoon (15 ml) rose water
- 1 pink candle
- 1 stick of rose incense

TIMING: Perform this ritual on a moonlit night.

Place all the oils, rose water, and aloe vera gel into your squeeze bottle. Shake the mixture well. As you undress, imagine you are preparing for the one you love. Light the pink candle and rose incense and say:

My heart is open, my spirit soars.

Goddess bring my love to me. Blessed be.

Now, pour the Oil of Love into your palm and gently rub into your skin. As you do so, dream of what delights are heading your way.

Ultimate Glamour

Few people know that the word "glamour" comes from the seventeenth-century Scottish word "glamour," which meant to cast a spell or enchantment over anyone who looks upon you. Carry out this spell before a date with a potential partner.

TIMING: This spell is best performed during the waxing moon.

Take the rings, necklace, and earrings you are planning to wear during your special tryst and lay them on your altar to imbue them with magic. Mix together one tablespoon each of the dried herbs vervain, thistle, chamomile, and elderflower. Cover your jewelry with the herb mixture and then sprinkle salt on top. Leave for at least 5 minutes, then shake off the herbs and pick up your gems.

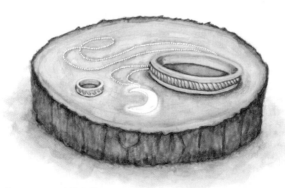

Hold the jewelry in your hands and chant:

Bless these jewels and the hand and heart of the wearer

With the light of heaven above.

May all who look upon me

See me through the eyes of love.

Now put on the empowered and enchanted jewelry and go off for your special date.

Quick Tip: *EARRING ALLEVIATION*
Wear one gold earring and one silver earring to rid yourself of the discomfort of a headache.

Twin-Hearts Candle Consecration

If you are seeking a soul mate, this simple spell will do the trick.

TIMING: Perform this spell on the next new moon.

Take two pieces of heart-shaped rose quartz and stand in the center of your bedroom. Light two pink candles and recite these words:

Beautiful crystal I hold this night,

Flame with love for my delight.

Harm to none as love comes to me.

This I ask and so shall it be.

Keep the candles and crystals on your bedside table and think of it as a shrine to love. Repeat three nights in a row and ready yourself for *amour*.

Flower Charm

This simple charm will help you open yourself up to love and new relationships.

TIMING: To light the flower of love in your heart, time this charm with the waning of a new Moon.

Place a green candle beside a white lily, rose, or freesia. Make sure it is a posy of personal preference. White flowers have the greatest perfume, and any one of these beauties will impart your home with a pleasing aura. I like to float a gardenia in a clear bowl of fresh water, truly the essence of the divine. Light the candle and hold the flower close to your heart. Pray using the spell:

Steer me to the highest light;

Guide me to beauty and truth.

Much have I to give. Much have I to live.

Bright blessings to one and all.

Spell for Letting Go

Most of us have had problems giving up on a relationship at one time or another. This rite can help you move on.

Gather together

- a piece of black string, enough to tie around your waist
- bolline (see page 144)
- a photo or memento representing your ex

TIMING: Ideally this should be done during the waning moon when things can be put to rest, but it works anytime you need it. Listen to your heart and you'll know exactly when it is required.

Tie the black string around your waist during the waning moon. Tie something symbolic from the old relationship to the end of the string—a photo or the name written on a scroll of paper, for example. Speak this spell aloud:

Bygones be and lovers part,

I'm asking you to leave my heart.

Go in peace, harm to none.

My new life is now begun.

Go outside and, using your sacred bolline, cut off the string and toss it away along with the memento where it will no longer inhabit your living space. You should feel freer and lighter immediately and will attract many new potential paramours now that you are not weighed down by lost love.

New Moon Charm for Banishing Heartbreak

Clear away relationship "baggage" with this banishing spell. If you have been hurt emotionally, this will clear it, fast.

Gather together

- a clear glass bowl filled with 2 cups (480 ml) of water
- silver spoon
- salt shaker
- palo santo incense
- 2 white candles and 2 black candles

TIMING: Any new moon is the perfect time to create a new opportunity.

Place the clear glass bowl of water on your altar. Set a silver spoon beside the glass bowl along with a salt shaker. Light the cleansing palo santo incense, the two white candles, and the two black candles. Pour salt on the spoon, sprinkle the salt into the water and stir with the spoon clockwise. Recite aloud:

Hurt and pain are banished this night;

Fill this heart and home with light.

With harm to none and blessings to all.

So mote it be.

After a few moments of contemplating the candle flames, recite the spell again. Using the silver spoon as a snuffer, extinguish the candles. Toss the bowl of water out on the street in front of your house, near a drainage grate. All your love troubles should drain away by the end of this lunar cycle.

Sensual Soak: Scorpio Moon Rite

Sandalwood, amber, and vetiver are all rich, earthy scents that combine well together and are used for these relaxing bath salts.

Gather together

- 5 drops sandalwood essential oil
- 5 drops amber essential oil
- 2 drops vetiver essential oil
- ½ cup (90 g) Epsom salts
- ½ cup (70 g) baking soda

TIMING: The moon in Scorpio is the time to explore bodily pleasures.

Combine the essential oils with the Epsom salts and stir in the baking soda. Mix well to create a richly scented paste. You can use a couple of different ways: either slather it onto yourself and shower off with a loofah and thick washcloth or, and this is my favorite way to soak up this earthly pleasure, roll it into a ball after you mix it and place under the faucet as you are running a hot bath. The entire room will smell like paradise. Soak it all in, lie back, and enjoy this fully.

If you want to keep this for the future or give as a thoughtful gift, you can store it in a lidded container or roll it into bath bombs and let them dry on wax paper or paper towels. This recipe can make three palm-size bath bombs. Note: you will be asked for more!

chapter 6

Divine Abundance

Manifesting with the moon

For centuries, witches have known that luck is neither random nor mysterious. Performing a spell at the optimal time in the lunar cycle will maximize your power. Thanks to the wise women in my family who shared their "trade secrets" openly, I learned very early in life that I could manifest what I wanted and needed through tools of magic and the moon. Keep this essential approach to magic in mind. When in a pinch, I have used witchcraft to replenish the coffers. I have also used prosperity spells to find a good home, attract job opportunities, and help others. Timing is everything!

Crescent Moon Magic

This is the perfect time to lay plans for all good things you desire in this phase of increasing.

Gather together

- pure white garment
- moonstone of any size
- short piece of string

TIMING: The ideal phase for this spell is when the crescent moon is waxing.

In the first quarter of the moon, don your white shirt or dress, and carry the moonstone along with you in your pocket or on a pendant. Take a late afternoon walk in a park or a meadow among wild weeds, flowers, and grasses, and gather a few as you stroll to make a bouquet. Choose a resting place and sit where you can see the crescent moon. Take your flowers and grasses and bind them with the string. Hold your newly made bouquet in your right hand. Hold your moonstone in your left hand and concentrate on your desired outcome—creative fulfillment, greater happiness, or perhaps the release of anger. Chant aloud:

Luna, in your seventh heaven, I invoke you now.

Brighter than any star, you are.

I will sing your magic song if you but show me how.

I will walk your sacred path if you but show me where.

Be here now.

Arms outspread, eyes on the moon, repeat the chant three times. As the moon shines brighter, so will your spirit.

Foretelling Your Future: Mercury Sortilege

The god Mercury prevails over communication, speed, prophecy, mental clarity, and fun. Traditionally, he also escorts the dead to the afterworld. All things yellow and citrus can bring forth Mercury's bright presence, which will help you in all your interactions with others. Try these surefire ways to make contact with the god of swiftness and time.

Gather together

- 3 yellow candles
- lemon essential oil
- neroli essential oil
- a notebook and a pen

TIMING: It is best to do this during the waxing moon.

When the moon begins to wax, burn all three candles. Anoint yourself and the candles with the essential oils. Look at the flames and meditate upon them. Breathe deeply, filling your lungs with the fiery citrus scent. Holding both hands out, palms up, say the words opposite.

Messenger of the gods,

Bring me your news.

Tonight, in this fire and flame,

Tell me the place and the name.

Mercury, messenger and god,

I will listen for your word on the wing.

Blessed be, to thee and me.

Now, you can either go to sleep with your dream journal nearby, or you can close your eyes and take up your pen for "automatic writing," allowing your hand and wrist to relax until you see what words take shape on the paper. Carefully record symbols and images that show up in your dreams; they all have meaning. Often, the names of people you will soon meet appear here first.

Coin Conjuration

We all have unexpected expenses that come out of the blue—car repairs, medical bills, or helping a loved one in need. I had the latter with my family and had to reach deep into my coffers to heed the call. When you need to recover quickly financially, this coin spell will fill the bill, literally.

Gather together

- athame (see page 144)
- 3 gold (or yellow) candles
- frankincense or myrrh incense
- 3 yellow or gold-colored crystals, such as tiger's eye, amber, citrine, yellow jade, or another favorite of yours
- 3 pieces of yellow- or gold-colored fruit, such as yellow apples or oranges
- 13 coins of different denominations
- a green or gold jar with a lid

TIMING: Perform this spell on the evening of a new moon or during a waxing moon phase.

Make a temporary altar wherever you pay your bills and handle your money—maybe it is your desk or perhaps the kitchen table. Use your athame to create the circle of magic in this soon-to-be-sacred space. Place the candles, incense, crystals, and fruit on the temporary altar and arrange them into three groups so each group contains a crystal, piece of fruit, and candle. Light your candles and the incense. One by one, take the coins in your hand and pass them through the incense smoke. Place the coins in the jar. Now take the crystals in your hand and pass them through the smoke, then place in the jar and seal. Pick up one piece of fruit at a time and touch to your third eye (in the middle of your forehead). Pray aloud:

This offering I make as my blessing to all,

Comfort and earthly gifts upon us shall fall.

Fill my coffers with silver and gold.

In this time of great need, I will be bold.

For the good of all, young and old.

Fill my coffers with silver and gold.

And so it is.

Extinguish the candles and incense and place on your altar for future use, as well as the vessel containing the coins. When you go to sleep, dream of everyone you love, including yourself, receiving a harvest of material and spiritual wealth.

Prophetic Pouch: Dianic Dream Divination

This charm will help you to see into your very recent past as well as your near future if you want to understand why you are having sleep disruptions or other issues that are causing upset, sleeplessness, and worry. Often, we might be surprised by what is causing our stress. It is important to figure it out so you can deal with it. Prepare this magical pouch for clairvoyance.

Gather together:

- lavender, mint, chamomile, and cloves
- 1 vanilla bean
- 3 cinnamon sticks
- jasmine essential oil
- small muslin bag or cloth pouch

TIMING: Perform any night before you go to sleep.

Stuff the bag with the herbs. Add the vanilla bean along with the cinnamon sticks, having placed a drop of jasmine oil on both. Tie up the pouch and hold it in both hands until your warmth and energy fully infuse the herbal potpourri mix. Say aloud:

Goddess Diana, Ruler of our Moon,

You are the huntress, brave and true.

Bring me my truth; may I know it soon,

Goddess le Lune; for these blessings from you.

And so it is. Blessed be thee.

Tuck your dream pouch into your pillowcase before bedtime. Have a pen and paper on the nightstand and on waking, record the night's dream. You will receive your answer immediately.

Unleash Your Visionary Powers

Mugwort has long been used in magical workings, starting in Mesopotamia and expanding throughout Europe, Asia, and now the world. It is used by seers and shamans for achieving new levels of consciousness. Mugwort is especially good for the mental plane and helps overcome headaches and soothes anxiety for mental balance and calm.

Gather together

- yellow candle
- stick of vanilla incense
- incense burner
- single yellow flower in a vase
- bowl
- citrine crystal
- 1 teaspoon dried mugwort

TIMING: Use this spell at any time you need to sharpen your sixth sense, which will guide you and enhance every aspect of your life.

Light the candle, and then light the stick of vanilla incense and place it in a fire-safe burner. Place the yellow flower and vase to one side of the incense burner. On the other side, place a bowl containing a citrine crystal. Yellow symbolizes intelligence and mental clarity. In your teakettle, boil the water. Pour it into the bowl, add the teaspoon of mugwort, and stir. Once it has cooled completely, dip your fingers in the water and touch your "third eye" at the center of your forehead. Now speak aloud:

Diana, Goddess of the Moon,

Fill me with your presence divine.

I seek your vision; lend me this boon.

Greatest seer, may the second sight be mine.

And so it is. And may it be soon.

After a few moments of contemplation, extinguish the candle. Your new psychic abilities will become apparent soon.

Lunar Birthday Spell

Your lunar birthday (see page 142) is a time to record your wishes for the year. Make the most of this day of enchantment by writing down your hopes and dreams on a sheet of white paper.

TIMING: Perform this on your lunar birthday.

Light lots of incense and candles on your altar—every candle is your birthday candle today. Begin by invoking the lunar deities of your choice from the list on the right, and speak this spell:

*I call upon the goddesses and gods of the moon,*_____ [list the deities you wish to call upon],

On this day, my personal new year,

Grant me the grace and wisdom I need.

Grant me the soul and spirit I need.

Grant me the health and wealth I need.

Bring me the love and happiness I desire.

Make my home and family safe.

Now read out your list of hopes and dreams, then speak this prayer of gratitude to the deities:

I thank you for all of your wisdom and grace,

With harm to none, so mote it be!

Tie your list of wishes and dreams into a scroll using colored string and place it on your altar. I leave my lunar birthday wish scroll on my home altar all year. I check it the following year, to see what came true, before tucking it into my Book of Shadows (see page 144). This ritual has become a touchstone for me, grounding and enriching the wheel of each 13-moon year.

MOON DEITIES OF THE WORLD

Call on any of these gods and goddesses, all of whom have an association with the moon within the religions and cultures that worship them, for your lunar magic:

Aah	Diana	Jacy	Mani	Sin
Anahita	Gou	Khonsu	Metztli	Soma
Artemis	Hathor	Kilya	Min	Tsukuyomi
Asherali	Hecate	Lucina	Nanna	Thoth
Astarte	Ilmaqah	Luna	Pah	Varuna
Baiame	Ishtar	Mah	Samna	Yarikh
Bendis	Isis	Mama Quilla	Selene	Yerak

chapter 7

Lunar Lore and Blessings

Essential celestial guidance

Our lives are basically a search for meaning and a personal ritual benefits you the most when it adapts to your current needs. You might notice you feel highly energetic one day and more laid back the next. Trust your intuition, go with your instincts, and listen to your heart. By following these three simple guidelines and synchronizing with the phases of the moon, you will craft beautiful, and more importantly, meaningful rituals to enrich your life, provide comfort, and maintain harmony and balance in your life.

Names for Full Moons

Many of our full-moon names come from medieval books of hours and also from the Native American tradition. Here is a list of rare names from the two traditions, which you may want to use in your lunar rituals.

January
Old Moon, Chaste Moon: This fierce Wolf Moon is the time to recognize your strength of spirit.

February
Hunger Moon: The cool Snow Moon is for personal vision and intention-setting.

March
Crust Moon, Sugar Moon: The gentle Sap Moon heralds the end of winter and nature's rebirth.

April
Sprouting Grass Moon, Egg Moon, Fish Moon: Spring's sweet Pink Moon celebrates health and full life force.

May
Milk Moon, Corn Planting Moon, Dyad Moon: The Flower Moon provides inspiration with the bloom of beauty.

June
Hor Moon, Rose Moon: The Strawberry Moon heralds the Summer Solstice and sustaining power of the sun.

July
Buck Moon, Hay Moon: This Thunder Moon showers us
with rain and cleansing storms.

August
Barley Moon, Wyrt Moon, Sturgeon Moon: Summer gifts us with the
Red Moon, the time for passion and lust for life.

September
Green Corn Moon, Wine Moon: Fall's Harvest Moon is the time to be
grateful and reap what we have sown.

October
*Dying Grass Moon, Travel Moon, Blood Moon, Moon of Changing
Seasons*; The Hunter's Moon is when we plan and store
for winter ahead.

November
Frost Moon, Snow Moon: Beaver Moon is the time to call upon
our true wild nature.

December
Cold Moon, Oak Moon: This is the lightest night of the shortest day
and is the time to gather the tribe around the fire and share stories
of the good life together.

Blissings Box: Herbs for Self-Love

Scent is such a powerful signal to the brain. Altars are perfect places to keep treasure boxes of ceremonial incenses and other sacred tools. In the following ritual, herbs and flowers remind you to hold yourself in the highest esteem, and every time you need a lift, you can open this box of bliss and breathe in pure love.

Gather together

- ¼ cup (5 g) pink rose petals
- ¼ cup (10 g) dried lavender
- ¼ cup (10 g) dried oregano
- small mixing bowl
- 3 drops lavender essential oil
- 3 drops rose essential oil
- small wooden box with lid
- pink jade, red jade, or rose quartz crystal

TIMING: Try to perform this rite during a new moon.

Place the flower petals and herbs into the bowl and gently mix together. Add the essential oils and mix again, then fill the box with the herbal mix. Settle the crystal in the herbs right at the top, then close the lid and place the box on your altar. Each night, open the box up and breathe in the lovely fragrance that will envelope you in an aura of love.

For Insights and Ideas: Element of Air Tonic

This spell should give you brilliant insight, enabling you to see with great peace and clarity.

Gather together

- 1 tablespoon fenugreek seeds
- 4 tablespoons fresh peppermint leaves
- a pinch of dried lavender
- a yellow teapot
- honey

TIMING: Perform this spell when the new moon is in an Air sign: Aquarius, Gemini, or Libra.

Steep the herbs in boiling water in your sunny yellow teapot; yellow is one of the colors associated with mental prowess. After 5 minutes, sweeten with honey, and either drink the mild tea while facing east, the source of the rising sun, or mark the four directions and pour the tea on the ground outside toward the east, praying:

Winged Mercury, God of air,

I entreat you to bring me sight and true awareness.

Like the wind, speed my way.

Make everything new.

Listen to your intuition now; it will not fail you.

Magic Amplified: Prayer for Pagan Partnership

Perhaps what you need most is a partner to support, encourage, and collaborate with in your magical workings. This spell will bring your partner to you. It uses rosemary, which has a very powerful cleansing smoke. It was used as an incense by ancient priests and priestesses in Greek and Roman times and by prophets and seers. It cleanses the aura and paves the way for major magic.

Gather together

- 1 lemon
- 1 orange
- 2 rosemary sprigs
- 1 orange candle
- fireproof clay or glass dish

TIMING: Perform on a waxing moon Friday night.

Group the fruit and rosemary around the orange candle.
Light the candle and intone:

On this night

I do invite

New energy to bring delight

Under this lunar light.

So mote it be.

Now, using the candle flame, light the tip of the rosemary sprigs
and set them in the fireproof dish. Soon your partner in spellwork
will appear.

Gratitude Prayer Spell

Gratitude is not only uplifting but feels wonderful. There is powerful magic in recognizing all that you possess.

TIMING: When the moon or sun is in the sign of Taurus it is the time of prosperity and security. Time this ritual for a Thursday during that lunar or solar sign as Thursday is "Thor's Day" and the day of abundance. It is also the perfect time to acknowledge the gifts of life.

Sit in a comfortable position and close your eyes. Think about your blessings. What are you grateful for at this moment? Breathe steadily and deeply, inhaling and exhaling slowly for a few minutes.

Now pray aloud:

Good gods and Goddess, giver of all the fruits of this earth,

Thank you for all bounty, beauty, and wellbeing,

Bless all who give and receive these gifts.

I am made of sacred earth, purest water, sacred fire, and wildest wind.

Blessings upon me. Blessings upon we and thee.

So mote it be.

Record your blessings in a journal or in your Book of Shadows (see page 144). You should perform this gratitude prayer spell periodically and look back at your blessings and reflect upon them. This is also a wonderful grace to say at the family meal to offer thanks for all we are given.

Guardian Moon Spell

This little spell will take you deep inside yourself. It will greatly empower you and instill in you a much deeper understanding of who you truly are and what you are here to do. Each of us is as individual as a snowflake, and our souls are imprinted with a stamp of specialness. The closer you get to the revelation of your soul's mission, the more you will know why you are here, and more importantly, what you are here to do. That is real magic.

TIMING: The best time to perform this spell is during the dark of the new moon, when the night sky is at its darkest. The new moon is also the best time for initiating the new in your life.

Gather together:

- compass
- athame (see page 144)
- 1 white votive candle and glass jar
- mint essential oil
- ginger, cardamom, allspice, nutmeg, or clove incense
- paper and pen

Go outside and find a solitary space in which you can use the compass to find true north. When you feel comfortable and safe to begin, cast a circle of energy by pointing your athame in all four directions, starting with north and moving clockwise, or sun-wise. Acknowledge each direction as you go and call in the spirit guardians.

Stand in the center of the circle, and with your forefinger, anoint your candle with the essence of mint, a herb that stays strong, green, and alive with healing energy. Place the candle in the glass jar and light it, setting the jar carefully and securely on the ground. Then light the incense with the flame of the candle and put it on the ground beside the candle.

Breathe slowly and deeply. Be mindful that you are here in the darkest night, celebrating the sacred. As you breathe, look around at the majesty of nature and the world around you. Feel the ground beneath your feet. Listen to the silence around you. Now open your heart completely to the awesome power of the universe and the magic both inside and outside of you.

With eyes closed, speak aloud:

Standing here beneath the moonless sky,

I open my heart and wonder why

I am here. What is my true north, my turn?

Tonight, I will learn

The reason why I yearn

To serve the Goddess and the God.

This night, I'll hear the reason

I serve this healing moon season.

Guardians, I call on you now!

You may hear an inner voice, or you may hear an outer voice right beside your ear. Listen calmly, staying centered with your two feet on the ground. You will know when it is time for you to leave with your new message and mission. Thank the guardians as you seal the sacred space, being sure to leave everything exactly as you found it. Incense, jar and candle, and matches should all leave with you. When you return home, write the message on a slip of paper and place it on your altar, where it will be hidden from any eyes but yours.

Place the candle in its jar and any remaining incense on your altar and burn them each dark moon night.

Here's a final thought. You may also want to begin a special journal of your thoughts, inspirations, and actions regarding the message you received. You have now embarked on an exciting new phase of your life's journey. Your journal will help you as you make discovery after discovery. It may evolve into a Book of Shadows (see page 144), or it may one day become a book like this!

Resources

YOUR LUNAR BIRTHDAY

We all know our birthday, but our lunar birthday in Western astrology is the one day of the year when the sun and moon are in exactly the signs they were on the wonderful day you were born. Your personal power is likely to be at its height on that day, so it is ideal for making magic. You probably already know your sun sign (sometimes called your star sign), but perhaps not your moon sign, and you will also need to know what degree the moon was in at the time you were born.

To find out your lunar birthday, check the position of the planets and stars in an ephemeris for the current year. The ephemeris may look complicated, but you need only look at the first three columns, which show the day of the month, the position of the sun, and the position of the moon. You will see that at some point near your birthday, the sun and moon will be in the same signs as when you were born. There may be a few days of crossover, but the one that is your lunar birthday is when the sun and moon are in the same degree or close to it (this is the first number shown in the sun and moon columns). Each year will vary slightly, and sometimes it will line up with the actual date of your birth.

ASTROLOGY

Cafe Astrology (www.cafeastrology.com) is a hugely useful site for all your astrology needs. Use the following links when working out your lunar birthday:
- To find out your sun sign:
www.cafeastrology.com/whats-my-sun-sign.html
- To find out your moon sign:
www.cafeastrology.com/whats-my-moon-sign.html
- To find the ephemeris for previous and upcoming years:
www.cafeastrology.com/ephemeris.html